NATIONAL GEOGRAPHIC

Ladders

Connections to Nature

GENRE Third-Person Narrative

Read to find out about John Muir and the Sierra Nevada.

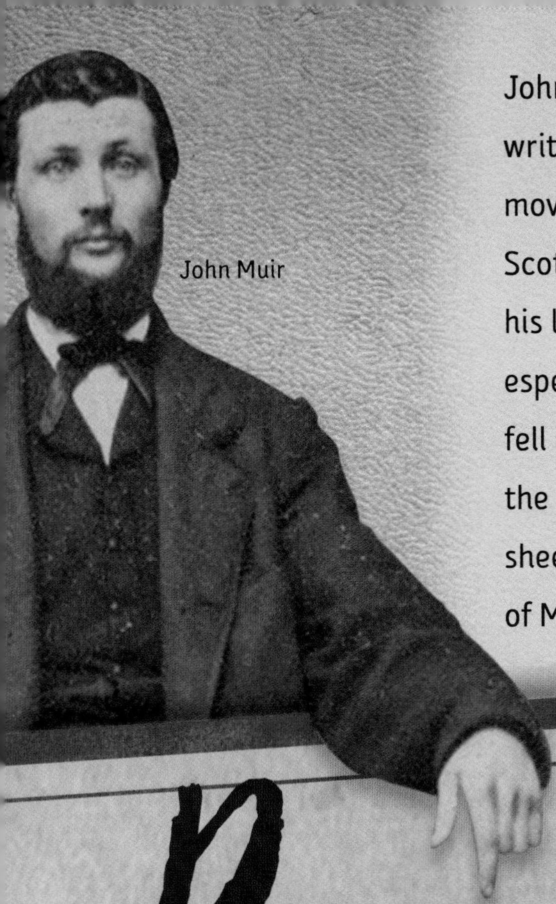

John Muir

John Muir was an avid **naturalist,** explorer, and writer who helped lead the early conservation movement in America. Although Muir was born in Scotland and traveled the world, he spent much of his life fighting to preserve the American wilderness, especially the Sierra Nevada of California. Muir fell in love with these mountains when he spent the summer exploring them while working as a sheepherder. That summer would shape the rest of Muir's personal and professional life.

Rambles

by Jennifer Boudart

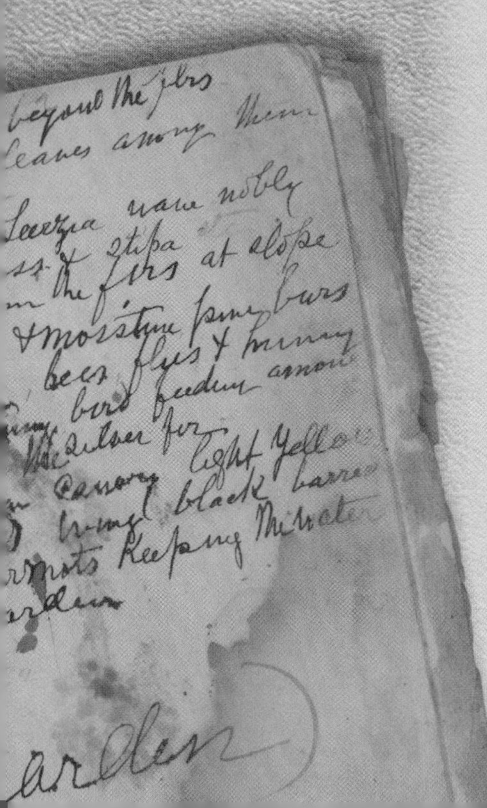

The 30-year-old Muir was already a seasoned outdoorsman. He had previously walked 1,609 kilometers (1,000 miles) from Indiana to the Gulf of Mexico and explored tropical forests in Cuba. In 1868, John Muir came to San Francisco, California, seeking "any place that is wild." Now Muir was anxious to find his way out of town. He set off by foot for Yosemite Valley, armed with a blanket, some tea and bread, a plant press, and a notebook. Muir was eager to see if Yosemite was as beautiful in reality as it had appeared in photos. He was indeed enchanted by his first sight of the valley, as well as the Sierra Nevada mountain **range,** which he came to call the "Range of Light."

Muir stayed in California and took a job with a rancher named Mr. Delaney. The young Scotsman dreamed of exploring the Sierras further, but he lacked money for such a trip. Muir's problem was solved when Delaney gave him new duties in the summer of 1869.

Muir would join a small party of men, a few dogs, and a flock of some 2,000 sheep as they made their way to high summer pastures above Yosemite Valley—exactly where Muir wished to go! Muir confessed he had little experience herding sheep. But Delaney assured him he had only to make sure the shepherd did his job. Beyond that, Muir would be free to explore the mountains, which Delaney knew were the young man's passion. So on June 3, the group set out: Muir, Delaney, Billy the shepherd, and two other ranch hands.

As Muir climbed with the flock toward higher **elevations,** the true grandeur of Yosemite began revealing itself. Muir explored canyons and caves and eyed the snowy peaks that marked the trail's end. On June 8, the group established their first base camp along the Merced River. There, the sheep would graze for the next month. Muir's camp duties included washing dishes, making bread, and finding lost sheep with the help of Carlo, a Saint Bernard dog loaned to him by a local hunter. His duties as a naturalist included studying wildlife, collecting plants, and filling his journal with sketches and notes. Muir sometimes encountered other people, including occasional tourists; local Indians; and ranchers, loggers, and miners. These early encounters with people using the land caused him concern over "scars" that human activities were leaving on the mountain **ecosystem**.

"Glorious days I'll have sketching, pressing plants, studying the wonderful topography . . ."

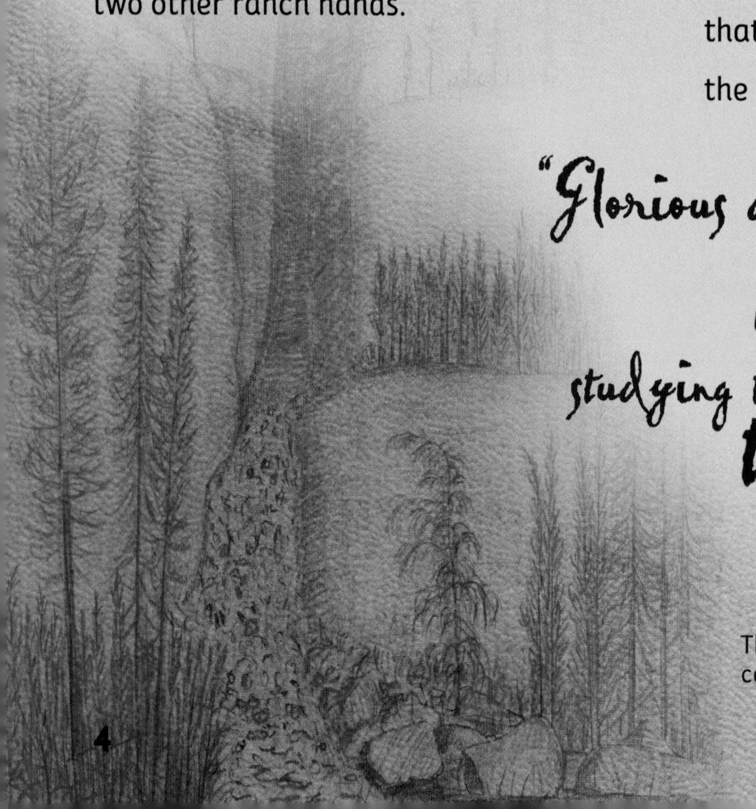

This is a sketch Muir drew of a canyon near Yosemite Valley.

The Merced River runs through Yosemite Valley.

Yosemite Falls

In early July, the group headed for a new camp. They followed the Yosemite Trail for a time, hiking at an elevation of 2,133 meters (7,000 feet). The grazing was good, and the sheep were allowed to eat and climb at their own pace among meadows and boulder fields. Muir was not a fan of sheep, which he called "silly," "woolly bundles," "busy nibblers," and "hoofed locusts." They were always getting stuck in bushes, running away, or balking at rivers, which terrified them. But thanks to them, he was able to take daily "rambles" on his beloved mountain range. Muir often chose curiosity over caution on these walks. For example, he actually tiptoed along a three-inch ledge to the very edge of Yosemite Falls. He put himself in the path of a bear. And he climbed to the top of Mount Hoffman, the highest he'd ever gone—about 3,352 meters (11,000 feet).

Mount Hoffman

One afternoon, Muir sat on the North Dome sketching, when he had a sudden vision of his old college professor staying at a hotel in the valley below him. His professor had mentioned a possible trip to Yosemite, but Muir had heard no further details from him. Even so, Muir immediately started scrambling down the mountain. After a few inquiries at the hotel, Muir did in fact track down his professor on a local trail, and they spent the day visiting!

"Ramble to the summit ... the highest point in life's journey my feet have yet touched."

Muir's sketch of Half Dome

In early August, bears attacked and killed a number of sheep. The group had to move up the Mono Trail to make their last camp at about 2,743 meters (9,000 feet) in the Tuolumne Meadows, along the Tuolumne River. Muir explored the woods, meadows, and nearby waterfalls, as well as Mono Lake and its surrounding desert. He climbed mountains named and unnamed, including Cathedral Peak (the first known ascent of that mountain). During this time, Muir became convinced that ancient **glaciers** had carved out Yosemite Valley. His theory differed from the then accepted claim that earthquakes had shaped the valley.

In early September, the group broke camp. The sheep had enjoyed excellent grazing, and to stay any longer was to risk getting caught in an early snowstorm. The group spent two weeks backtracking down to the foothills, past all the old camps, forcing the sheep across the same waterways.

Cathedral Peak

The weather was cooling, the rivers were dropping, the berries were ripening, and the grasses were dying. Summer was over. At trail's end, they counted the sheep. Only thirteen were lost due to predators, injury, or running away. Three were sold to other ranchers. Nine became camp food. Muir had faced bears, starvation, bloodthirsty mosquitoes, severe weather, and dangerous heights. And he had loved every minute of it. Muir's last journal entry told of his hope to experience the grandeur of the High Sierra again.

"I have crossed the Range of Light."

Muir's sketch of himself on one of his "rambles"

Muir described Tuolumne Meadows as a "flowery carpeted mountain hall."

Muir made this sketch showing how retreating glaciers chiseled away at the granite features of Yosemite Valley.

"Unless reserved or protected the whole region will soon or late be devastated . . ."

Theodore Roosevelt (left) admired Muir and sought him out as a guide to Yosemite Valley.

John Muir did see more of his beloved mountains. He went to work at a sawmill on the banks of Yosemite Creek. For two years, Muir lived in a cabin he'd built at one end of the sawmill. Muir set the cabin high on stilts, then diverted water from the creek so it flowed under his cabin where he could hear it. He spent every free moment exploring the Sierra, looking for evidence that glaciers had formed Yosemite Valley.

In 1871, Muir found an active glacier (one that retreats and advances) high in the mountains and published an article about it. He soon became known as an expert on Yosemite. He moved away from the area in 1874, but in the years that followed, he wrote numerous articles about threats to the region, especially logging and ranching. He also campaigned for the protection of other wilderness areas throughout the country.

Photo of Yosemite Falls in Yosemite Valley, 21st Century

In 1889, Muir wrote a series of articles highlighting the damage sheep were causing to Yosemite's ecosystem. Muir called on Congress to preserve Yosemite's unique landscape by making it a national park. His efforts paid off. Parts of the Yosemite region became a national park in 1890. However, Yosemite Valley and a nearby grove of giant sequoia trees were not included. When President Theodore Roosevelt took a three-day camping trip in Yosemite with Muir in 1903, the naturalist persuaded Roosevelt to add these areas to the park. Muir was also instrumental in establishing other national parks, as well as a conservation group he named the Sierra Club, which still operates today. He wrote numerous articles and books over the next 25 years and continued to be a voice for conservation right up to the time of his death at age 76.

Check In How did John Muir's exploration in California impact the rest of his life?

GENRE Personal Narrative

Read to find out about one man's hike in northern California.

Wiffle® Chicken's Hike

by Mike McDonald

July 1–4 Mount Whitney, California

My name is Mike, and I'm a long-distance hiker. Out on the trail, I'm known as *Wiffle Chicken*. Trail names are part of the culture of long-distance hikers. In part, my trail name comes from my love of baseball and my days playing on my college team. I like baseball so much, I brought a Wiffle ball and bat on my hike. And the chicken part? Well, that was just for fun.

From July 1 to July 15, 2010, I hiked along the John Muir Trail in northern California. This trail is named in honor of the great **naturalist** and explorer, John Muir. My journey along this trail was part of a longer hike along the Pacific Crest Trail, which begins at the border of Mexico.

Mount Whitney is 4,421 meters (14,505 feet) above sea level.

Mike's Hike on the John Muir Trail

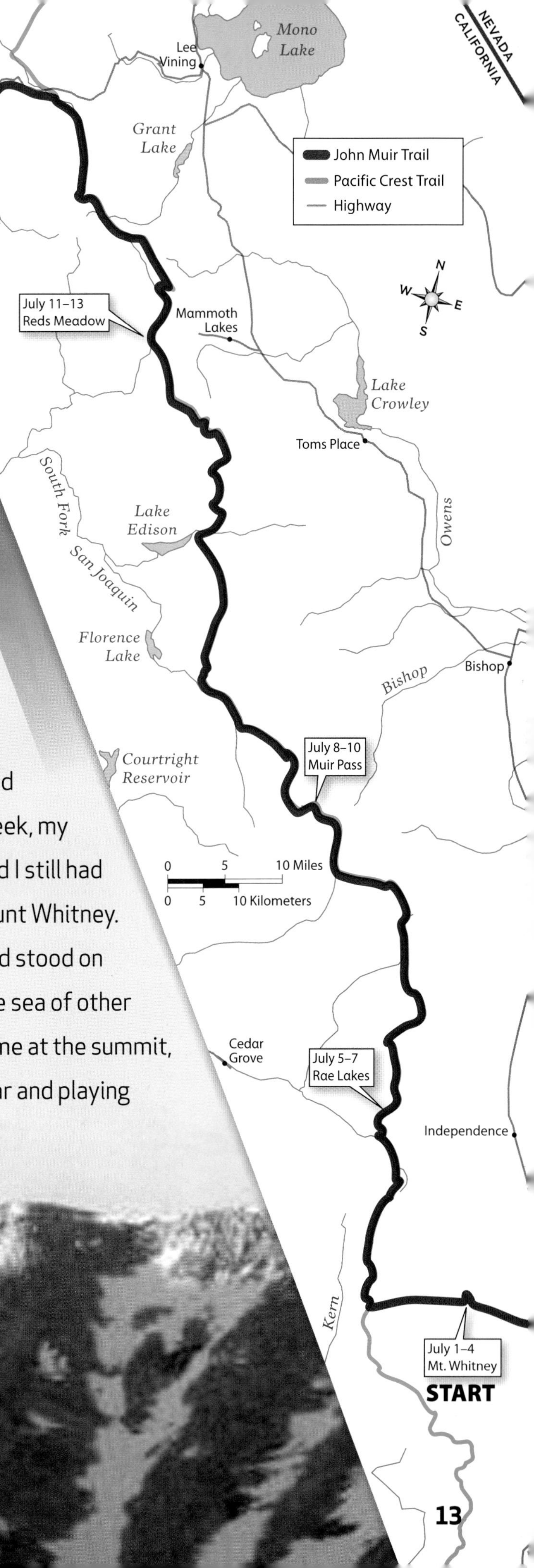

By the time I reached the John Muir Trail, I had been hiking for 44 days. I had already worn through two pairs of shoes.

On July 1, I woke at 5:30 AM to start my hike. The summit of Mount Whitney marks the beginning of the John Muir Trail, which runs 339.5 kilometers (211 miles) through the Sierra Nevada mountain **range.** Mount Whitney is often considered the highlight of the entire Pacific Crest Trail. Before much time had passed, I faced an icy cold creek that I would have to **ford,** or cross. After fording the creek, my feet were wet, and my toes were numb. And I still had a long way to climb to get to the top of Mount Whitney. At 10:30 AM, I reached its rocky summit and stood on the massive **granite** slabs to look out at the sea of other mountain peaks. Soon other hikers joined me at the summit, and we celebrated by eating a chocolate bar and playing a quick game of Wiffle ball.

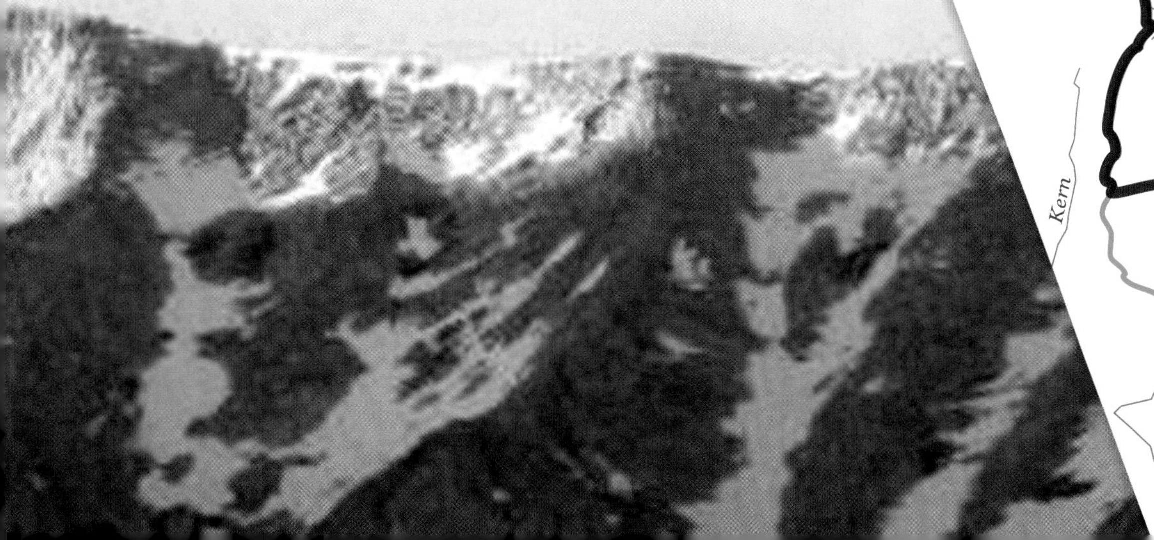

July 5–7 Rae Lakes

On July 5, I reached the Rae Lakes with my hiking friend, Breezy. The lakes were set among bright, green, grassy meadows. A few scattered pine and fir trees stood around the shore. The view was stunning. Massive snow-topped granite peaks towered above the sparkling, blue water of the lakes.

Breezy and I forded the wide creek and stood with sopping wet shoes on the other side. Another hiker, Cheeseburger, wanted to avoid getting his shoes wet.

If you were to hike around the Rae Lakes, you would travel 74 meters (46 miles).

So he decided to take off his shoes and throw them across the creek. Just like a baseball pitcher, he wound up and threw his first shoe over his head, and it landed with a thud on the creek bank. He boldly launched his second shoe directly into the middle of the creek's swift current. Always quick to help, Breezy reacted at once. He dropped his backpack and sprinted down the trail as fast as his feet would carry him. He jumped into the middle of the creek and managed to grab the runaway shoe. Cheeseburger sheepishly grinned. He realized he easily could have been many miles away from civilization with only one shoe to wear.

What else was in my pack?

When hiking, every ounce in a pack adds up. It can start to feel like you are carrying an elephant on your back after a few miles of hiking. When I started the John Muir Trail, this is what was in my pack:

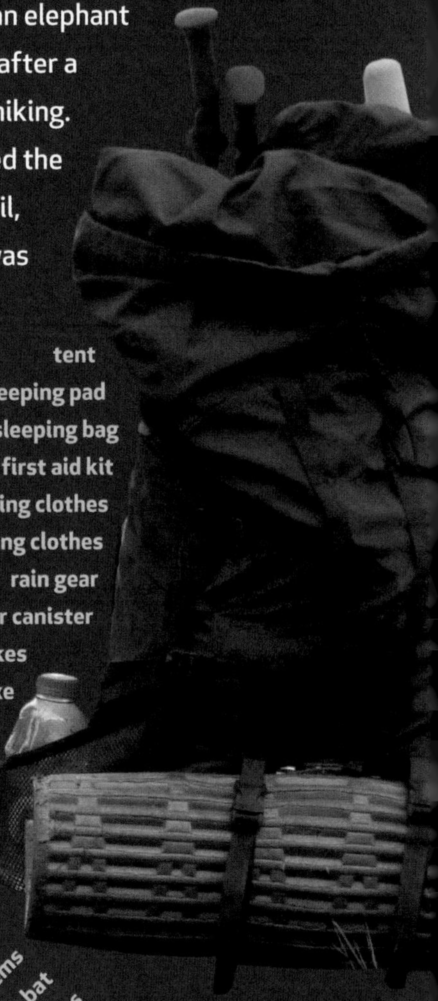

tent
sleeping pad
sleeping bag
first aid kit
hiking clothes
sleeping clothes
rain gear
bear canister
shoe micro spikes
ice axe
water filter
food
water bottles
maps
compass
pen
journal pages
toiletry items
Wiffle ball & bat
flip flops

My backpack and gear alone weighed **18** pounds

+ 34 pounds of food

52 pounds

To help with the weight, I carried only a few pages of my map book and a paperback book of short stories to read when I rested. But it was just half of the book. My friend, Swiss Miss, carried the other half.

July 8–10 Muir Pass

On July 8, we hiked on from the Rae Lakes, heading toward Muir Pass. We had one more night sleeping under the cover of a few pine trees. But soon we had climbed to an **elevation** of about 3,048 meters (over 10,000 feet), and there were no more trees. The snow covered everything except the gray, granite rocks. The rocks had such a steep angle that the snow didn't stick to their surfaces. Here, the sound of trickling water flowing down the mountain slope told us that nearby snow was melting.

The higher we climbed, the more snow-covered the trail became. No melting had taken place, even in the middle of the California summer. We struggled to find the trail to Muir Pass. We looked for footprints of other hikers and used our map and compass to recognize landmarks in the area. We recognized Helen Lake, named after one of Muir's daughters. The lake's size and shape matched the map, and we knew we were near our goal. Soon we reached a stone hut at the top of Muir Pass. It was a great spot to admire the turquoise blue lakes dotting the massive snowfield spread out before us.

Once again the realities of hiking distracted me from the beautiful scenery. I noticed my trail running shoes had a small tear in the mesh. They were already quite well worn. Disaster struck when I stepped over a branch and the mesh of my shoe snagged on the branch. The small rip in my shoe tore open into a huge hole all the way to the sole of the shoe. I stopped to fix the shoe using what materials I had. I applied duct tape, sewed stitches with a needle and dental floss, and used safety pins to close the gaping hole. Then I was ready for more miles.

This stone hut, known as Muir Hut, is a welcome shelter for hikers.

July 11–13 Reds Meadow

From Muir Pass we descended into an area plentiful with fir trees. Now at just over 2,133 meters (7,000 feet) above sea level, the snow had vanished. It was nice to have softer dirt under our feet instead of the hard rocks and crunchy snow. It was July 11, and it felt as if we walked right out of one season and into another.

Reds Meadow was an area filled with wildlife. As an amateur naturalist, I loved any encounter with wildlife, and that day I heard "Eek! eek! eek!" I stopped and waited. I saw a flash of fur cross the trail. "Eek! eek! eek!" I kept very still. Suddenly, a mouse ran out of the bushes and streaked across the trail, nearly crossing my feet. Right behind the mouse

An alpine lake near Reds Meadow

raced a slender, agile, weasel-like creature —a pine marten. With automatic animal instinct, the pine marten pounced on the mouse. The mouse dangled from its mouth, and the pine marten looked at me, turned, and ran down the trail. It looked back once more as if to say, "That's how it's done, Wiffle Chicken!" before it leaped over a log and disappeared into the bushes.

It was shortly after that when I saw bear footprints in the dirt and scratch marks on a decaying log. The marks on the log were a sign that a hungry bear had been digging for insects. For the next few nights, I was careful to store my food properly so the bears would stay wild and not become a nuisance trying to get human food.

A Belly Full

Hikers need to eat nutritious foods that are rich in calories to supply their bodies with enough energy to exercise all day long. When the weather is colder, hikers need even more calories to keep warm. I estimated that I ate around 6,000 calories a day. This is 3 times the recommended daily allowance of 2,000 calories. Think of it like this:

If that was all I ate, I would have eaten at least 15 sandwiches and 20 apples every day to get enough calories!

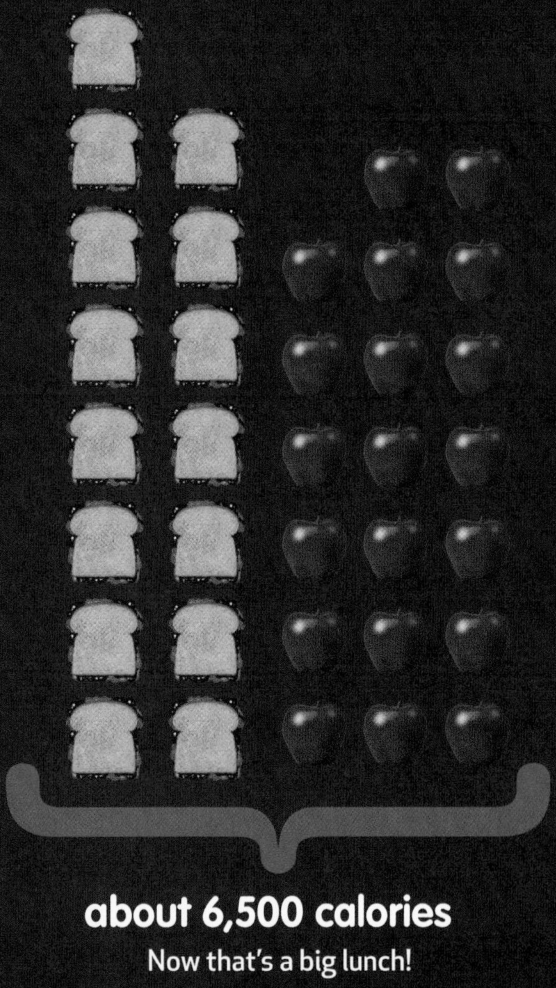

July 14–15 Yosemite Valley

The John Muir Trail continued to descend even lower, and it would be only a day until we reached Yosemite Valley, the end of the trail. It was along this stretch of trail that I noticed the clouds were increasing and the sky was getting darker. I heard the far-off booming of thunder and saw lightning snaking across the sky, getting closer and closer. An electrical storm passed and I was relieved I had not been turned into a toasted marshmallow. I walked the last few miles into Tuolumne Meadows. The meadows were an oasis of green surrounded by the awesome mountains.

A day later, on July 15, my hiking friend Swiss Miss and I covered the final stretch of the John Muir Trail. We hiked past the tops of two powerful waterfalls as the Merced River tumbled over the valley wall and fell hundreds of feet into Yosemite Valley. In the valley, crowds of people had flocked to see the huge waterfalls. Then

as part of the return to civilization, we enjoyed an extra large pizza, milk shakes, and rested our tired feet. My hiking companions and I had walked for 15 days, covering 339.5 kilometers (211 miles) beginning at 4,417 meters (14,494 feet) above sea level and ending in the valley, Muir's beloved valley, at 1,219 meters (4,000 feet) above sea level.

A day after completing the John Muir Trail, I hiked north to continue my journey on the Pacific Crest Trail. I continued the trek northward through rain, snow, and sunshine. I ended up seeing much more wildlife, large and small, including 14 bears and a few pesky mice. On October 9, after seven pairs of shoes and 4,264 kilometers (2,650 miles) of hiking, I completed the Pacific Crest Trail and crossed the Canadian border. My hike had touched the borders of three countries, Mexico, the United States, and Canada. I had crossed the states of California, Oregon, and Washington.

Later that autumn, I returned to San Francisco. I now live in Oakland, California, not too far from where John Muir himself settled after his glorious summer of exploring the Sierras. I am back at work in the city but have maps spread out all over my kitchen table, dreaming about where my next long hike will take me.

The upper waterfall of Yosemite Falls

Check In What parts of Mike McDonald's hike seemed to be the hardest?

GENRE Reference Article | **Read to find out** about plants and animals in Yosemite National Park.

IN THE ZONES

by Jennifer Boudart

A Guide to Yosemite National Park

Welcome to Yosemite, one of America's oldest and most stunning national parks. Spanning about 1,900 kilometers (1,200 square miles), Yosemite contains towering rock formations, rushing rivers and waterfalls, lush valleys, barren mountain peaks, even glaciers. In fact, ancient glaciers helped shape Yosemite, as slow-moving sheets of ice carved out the valley and its surrounding rock walls. The **elevation** in Yosemite varies dramatically, from about 550 meters to 3,962 meters above sea level (1,800–13,000 feet) and includes part of the Sierra Nevada mountain **range.** As elevation changes, the landscape and its mix of plants and animals changes, too. This results in a rich diversity of life. Because Yosemite is home—in some cases, the only home—to hundreds of animal **species** and more than a thousand plant species, a hiker, or even an experienced **naturalist,** should visit Yosemite with a field guide. A field guide will help identify the plants and animals in an area. The plants and animals in Yosemite occupy five main habitat zones. Each habitat occurs within a specific zone.

Visitors can access all five habitat zones in Yosemite.

482 Nearly 482 km (300 mi) of roads

1,287 about 1,287 km (800 mi) of hiking trails

Trails lead the way to waterfalls tucked into the foothills around Hetch Hetchy.

▼ The grey fox lives and hunts alone. It often takes refuge in thick chaparral.

▲ Whiteleaf manzanita is a chaparral shrub. Its thick, waxy leaves and red bark make it easy to identify.

▲ The blue oak does in fact have bluish-green leaves. Its acorns were once a favorite food of Native Americans living in the area.

► The mule deer is a common mammal in Yosemite, and it is the only species of deer found in the park.

Low Going Foothills
549–914 meters (1,800–3,000 feet)

FOOTHILL WOODLAND ZONE

Most visitors enter Yosemite National Park from the west, along Highway 140. The highway is open year-round, because this boundary of the park is at a low elevation. Very little snow falls here in winter, and summers are hot and dry. The highway takes visitors through the foothill woodland zone on its way to Yosemite Valley.

Trees in this zone are mainly species of oak. Shrubby plants also cling to the steep, rocky hillsides here, forming dense thickets called chaparral. Foothill woodlands also occur in the northwest corner of the park, near the Hetch Hetchy Reservoir. People hiking in this zone often see big mammals, such as black bears and mule deer.

▲ Most black bears living in Yosemite are more brown than black. Hikers are safe watching these bears from a distance but should never try to feed them.

Mariposa Grove is located at an elevation of nearly 6,000 feet.

▲ Several unique sequoias grow in Mariposa Grove. One sequoia, the Grizzly Giant, is thought to be almost 2,000 years old.

▼ The Douglas fir has needles, but it is not a true fir tree. Its cones do not match the cones of true fir trees.

The solitary bobcat defends its territory most actively at dawn and dusk.

Trees of Majesty

914–1,829 meters (3,000–6,000 feet)

LOWER MONTANE ZONE

Above the foothills on the western side of Yosemite, visitors enter the lower **montane** zone. *Montane* means "of the mountains," and this zone definitely has a mountain feel. Visitors can get more expansive views of nearby ridges and canyons. At this higher elevation, winter often brings several feet of snow. The lower montane zone has the biggest variety of plant life. Its forests include both deciduous trees, which shed their leaves, and **conifer** trees, which grow needle-like leaves year round. There are grassy meadows and some chaparral, too. The "stars" of the lower montane zone are the giant sequoias. These conifers represent Yosemite's biggest, oldest trees. The park's largest stand of sequoias—more than 500—is located in Mariposa Grove.

▶ The Sierra mountain kingsnake is not venomous and won't hurt people. However, it does eat rattlesnakes and is immune to their venom.

▼ Hikers may hear rather than see the elusive spotted owl. Its four-note call sounds like "hup, hoo-hoo, hooo."

▲ The Jeffrey pine's bark has a vanilla-like scent! It grows in exposed areas.

▼ The Sierra fence lizard is Yosemite's most visible reptile. Its behavior includes doing "push ups" to impress other lizards!

▼ The red fir's cones measure nine inches long. Cones don't drop off but instead disintegrate to release seeds.

▲ Lodgepole pinecones actually need fire to reproduce. Fire melts the cones' sticky coating, causing them to open and release seeds.

► Ostrander Lake is in the upper montane zone. Portions of surrounding lodgepole pine forest are fairly young because they're recovering from fires in 1987 and 1994.

Crowned with Conifers

1,829–2,438 meters (6,000–8,000 feet)

UPPER MONTANE ZONE

Conifers are kings of the forest above 1,829 meters (6,000 feet), where the upper montane zone begins. Conifer trees have needle-shaped leaves, which they replace a few at a time over the course of the year. Many people call them "evergreens." Trees of the upper montane zone mainly include species of fir, pine, hemlock, and juniper. These trees are designed to survive a short, cool growing season and cold winters with heavy snow. Wet bogs do break up the forest here and there, along with flowering meadows. Golden-mantled ground squirrels and blue grouse scurry across the forest floor. Porcupines and great gray owls seek shelter in the treetops.

▶ The golden-mantled ground squirrel resembles a chipmunk. It has a yellow-brown patch, or "mantle," on its neck and shoulders.

Tree Lines

2,438–2,896 meters (8,000–9,500 feet)

SUBALPINE ZONE

The subalpine zone is the highest elevation at which trees can grow. Winters here are extremely long, cold, and snowy. Trees often grow at odd angles, which helps them withstand strong winds. This zone also includes grassy meadows. Some of the park's most secretive creatures roam here, including mountain lions and Sierra Nevada bighorn sheep.

◀ The alpine chipmunk is active by day, foraging for seeds and fungi. It stores away its food for winter.

Tuolumne Meadows perches at 2,621 meters (8,600 feet). Only one road provides access, and for almost half of the year, the area is closed because of snow.

▼ Sierra Nevada bighorn sheep are an endangered species. Consequently, hikers rarely see them.

Rocky Tops

above 2,896 meters (9,500 feet)

ALPINE ZONE

Life is harsh but beautiful in the alpine zone. Shrubs poke up from the thin soil between boulders and exposed cliff tops. Wildflowers and numerous alpine butterflies flourish here in summer. Many alpine areas can only be reached by hiking into Yosemite's backcountry, beyond roads and established trails.

◀ The Sierra skipper is one of approximately 60 butterfly species found above 3,048 meters (10,000 feet). Females deposit their eggs on alpine grasses.

Many species of monkeyflowers flourish at various elevations in Yosemite. This mountain monkeyflower dots alpine meadows.

▼ Hikers may spot yellow-bellied marmots sunbathing on rocks. These large rodents form colonies.

Check In How does the zone at the lowest elevation differ from the zone at the highest elevation?

Discuss Information from the Past and Present

1. Why do you think the three pieces in this book relate to the theme of *Connections to Nature*?

2. The first two pieces take place in the same area. How are the two accounts alike and different?

3. In the first account, John Muir takes a short trip into the Sierra Nevada. How does his first trip affect the plans he makes after that?

4. What did you find most interesting about Wiffle Chicken's hike?

5. Think about the information you read about the Sierra Nevada mountain range and Yosemite National Park. Describe the geography of the area. How does the geography impact the plant and animal life?

6. What do you still wonder about Yosemite National Park? What would you like to learn more about?